CREATE YOUR MILLIONAIRE MINDSET

Attracting Everything You Want in Business and Life

Tim Campsall

Author: Tim Campsall

Cover and Interior Design: Fresh Design, Inc. Printed in the United States of America

Contents

Dedication

This book is dedicated to my amazing wife Petrita who has been my rock and support through my own mindset journey. Thank you for believing in me - I love you!

Foreword

By Brad Sugars, CEO of ActionCOACH

What does success mean to you? When pressed, I've found many people's concept of success is just the generalized idea of "being better." They visualize success as this vague place in the distance where life is easier, and things aren't as stressful. However, many business owners struggle to reach this ideal. When you think about it, this makes a lot of sense. How can you expect to accomplish a goal when you can't even define it?

I first noticed this problem when I was in my 20s. I ran a photocopy business and worked primarily with small businesses, so I noticed when I lost a customer because they went out of business. I realized these businesses had all the means to succeed, and the owners just needed a little coaching. So, I decided to teach them how to grow their businesses, which eventually inspired me to create ActionCOACH. Simply put, ActionCOACH's purpose is to help people achieve their dreams.

Like me, Tim Campsall became a business coach because he is passionate about helping others succeed. After years of coaching his teams and colleagues in the corporate world, Tim realized there had to be a better way to help more people. So, Tim left his corporate career to start his own ActionCOACH franchise. I was very excited to hear that Tim had written a book about mindset as that is a huge component to success in business.

Whether you are a top executive in a Fortune 500 company or a new small-business owner just getting started, you will benefit from implementing the knowledge found in this book. There is something new here for everyone, information that will make your life happier and more fulfilling. In addition, the advice presented in Tim's book is tried and tested by personal experience.

Keep an open mind and pay attention to the strategies he talks about in here. Listen to his advice and try it out in your own life. Tim is teaching you the same strategies I have been using throughout my 30-year career, and I'm now the CEO of an award-winning global franchise. The results speak for themselves.

Use the information and exercises provided to your advantage. It will help you visualize what success means to you, and then it will help you make it a reality. If you put in the time and energy, this book will hand you a road map to the success you have always dreamed of. If you learn to work smarter instead of just harder and stay committed to the principles in Tim's book, I promise you will start seeing significant results within a couple of weeks.

Your success is waiting for you, and I for one can't wait to see what you achieve.

Prologue

efore starting my business, I worked in the corporate world. I had a successful career; I climbed the ranks and was sought after by headhunters for opportunities at other companies. I worked for several major family-owned companies such as SC Johnson, Sargento Cheese, and Red Gold.

I was successful, but I longed for more. I was making a lot of money, but I was not fulfilled. There was something inside me that wanted something more. I thought it was simply wanting to keep growing in my corporate career, be promoted, and take on more responsibility. But after each big promotion that feeling always came back. *I wasn't making a difference.*

I had a wake-up moment in the fall of 2018, shortly after another big promotion that had me starting a new job in a new state. I was commuting back and forth on the weekends between states as I've done several times before, waiting for the summer when my family would be able to join me. It quickly became apparent that the new company was not a good fit for me. I chased the money and promotion, but I felt like a fish out of water. That is when I was forced to dig deep down inside and ask myself what I really wanted. *That is when I was forced to make a choice.*

I knew I had to leave that company, but should I continue to make the "safe" choice and work in another corporate setting?

The job hunt cycle was familiar to me, and I was good at it. The changes involved in moving were nothing my family and I had not handled before.

Or should I take charge of my life and pursue my dreams? I've always wanted to own my own business, but I had been too afraid to take the leap. The golden handcuffs of my corporate career were very hard to walk away from.

After a lot of soul searching, prayer, and many conversations with my wife, we decided that I would always regret not taking the opportunity to follow my passion. So, I quit my job and began chasing my dream of being a business owner.

I was first introduced to the ActionCOACH franchise in 2018 while doing research on business-to-business franchises. I didn't know that business coaching was a thing, but once I learned about it, I knew immediately that it is what I am meant to be doing.

In many ways, becoming a business coach was the natural next step for me. You see, we didn't have a lot of money when I was growing up. I didn't realize it at the time because we always did fun things as a family, and I never really wanted for anything. At least until the kids at school teased me for not having brand-name shoes and clothes. On top of that, I was also picked on for being overweight. This left a scar inside me that still surfaces today as a feeling of not being good enough, not being accepted, and not fitting in.

My need for acceptance and belonging combined with my fear of rejection has led me to keep pushing myself to excel in my career to 'prove myself.' It also has led me to make poor decisions to escape the pain and loneliness that I've felt. I was in my 30s when I came to know Jesus Christ as my Lord and Savior, and it has had an incredible life-changing impact on me.

As a result of all of my experiences, I have always had a passion for helping other people. I was a peer counselor in high school, a lay counselor at church, a Big Brother for a number of years, and I both donate and serve at the Rescue Mission to help people who have been underserved. Professionally my career was centered around it as well, as my desire to help my team become better versions of themselves was always stronger than the desire to be recognized.

Deep down, I think I've always known that helping other people achieve their full potential is my true calling. After I learned that I could do that through ActionCOACH, my path forward became clear to me. Purchasing an ActionCOACH franchise allowed me to be my own boss and run my own business, while still being a part of a larger network of people like me who have a passion for helping others.

I'm not going to pretend this has been easy. Truthfully, my business owner journey has been very difficult. There have been times I almost ran out of money, times when I was paralyzed with fear of failing, times I've cried uncontrollably when nothing seemed to be working, and times when I just wanted to throw in the towel and give up. I knew my mindset was holding me back, but I didn't really know how to change it.

Luckily, my approach to success was revolutionized in February of 2021 when I joined a mindset coaching program called Quality Minds. Thanks to Bruce Wilson, my mindset coach, I have discovered that my mindset has an even bigger impact on my business and my life than I had ever imagined. In fact, I've mapped out my business revenue over the past couple of years and I can see a 100% correlation between my mindset and my business results. For example, I've recently had a period of nine months in a row where I was pulling in personal record-breaking revenue at the end of every month. My mindset was strong and so were my profits. But then my self-limiting beliefs were triggered, my mindset suffered, and my revenue dropped by almost 50%.

My mindset journey is far from complete, I'm learning more every day. The strategies I'm sharing in this book are genuinely the strategies I use every day to make my own business successful and to help my clients with their businesses.

I used to think this stuff was a load of phooey but having been on this mindset journey with Bruce over the past two years,

I've come to know that this stuff really works! And I'm thrilled to share it with you, so that you can achieve success too.

"To me, the function and duty of a quality human being is the sincere and honest development of one's potential."

-   Bruce Lee

#1

Waking Up To Your Greatness

What if I told you that you have the ability to make as much money as you want? And what would you say if I told you that having more money is less about changing the way you work and more about changing the way you think?

Would you say I was crazy? Off my rocker? Not making any sense?

I certainly understand that. After all, we've been told our entire lives that the only way to have more money is to either:

Win the lottery

or

Work harder

The odds of you winning the lottery are small –you are more likely to get struck by lightning than win the lottery! So, if you really want to be successful, you can't rely on luck. There are much better ways to make money.

And while there's certainly some truth that you must work hard if you want money, you can have as much money as you want without necessarily working harder. Yes, for real!

See, here is the thing…

There is not a direct correlation between how hard you work and how much money you make.

Especially if you work for a salary. After all, plenty of people work incredibly hard and are lucky to get a 3% raise every year.

No matter how hard you work at your job, you're still going to be limited by your salary. You are also limited by time. There are only 24 hours in a day after all, and even the most driven of us have to sleep at some point.

This may seem to contradict what you have been taught up until this point, but it's true.

Hard work doesn't guarantee wealth, but there is a direct correlation between your money mindset and how much money you make.

In other words, the way you think about money has a real and direct influence on how much money you actually make.

Your money mindset can either:

Catapult you to wealth

or

Keep you in poverty

It is really that powerful.

This is why most people never reach the level of success they truly want. They've done things a certain way for so long that they can't see any other way of doing them. As a result, they have a limited mindset about achieving success and gaining wealth.

They're trapped where they are and don't know how to change.

In his book Secrets of The Millionaire Mind, T. Harv Ecker says:

> The reality is that most people do not reach their full potential. Most people are not successful. Research shows that 80 percent of individuals will never be financially free in the way they'd like to be, and 80 percent will never claim to be truly happy. The reason is simple. Most people are unconscious. They are a little asleep at the wheel. They work and think on a superficial level of life—based only on what they can see. They live strictly in the visible world.

Does this sound like you?

- Financially restricted?
- Unhappy in your day-to-day life?
- Asleep at the wheel?
- Just trying to make it through the day?

Deep down, you know that you should be achieving great things…

…but you just can't quite seem to get there.

If so, then this book is for you.

By teaching you how to reshape your thinking, this book will teach you how to truly change your life.

The only prerequisite for reading this book is an open mind.

Some of what you are about to read may contradict beliefs you have held about yourself and money for a long time. If you give these new ideas a chance, you will find that your old beliefs have been holding you back from reaching your true potential.

It's time for those beliefs to be put to rest and for you to embrace the true reality of who you are.

It's time to stop being unconscious - asleep at the wheel - and to wake up to your greatness.

Ready?

Let's get started.

"Beware of false knowledge; it is more dangerous than ignorance."

- George Bernard Shaw

#2

Myths You've Believed About Money

There's a good chance that what you believe about money is simply wrong. We've been conditioned by society, by our parents, and by our friends to believe certain things about money.

And most of us have believed those things without EVER questioning them.

Again, to quote T. Harv Ecker:

> You were taught how to think and act when it comes to money. These teachings become your conditioning, which becomes automatic responses that run you for the rest of your life. Unless, of course, you intercede and revise your mind's money files.

As a result of these unquestioned beliefs, many of us have what you might call a "difficult" relationship with money:

- We want more of it but can't ever seem to get enough.
- We know that money can achieve good things, but we feel conflicted when we spend it.
- We're grateful when we have the money to purchase the things we want, but we also feel like we're being selfish.

Why do we have this relationship with money? Why do we get so tied up in knots over it? Why do we stress about it so much?

It's because we've believed a lot of myths and lies about money and never questioned our beliefs to see if they are actually true.

And because we've never questioned them, we haven't achieved the level of success that we truly want.

In her book You Are A Badass At Making Money, Jen Sincero says:

> Our beliefs, along with our thoughts and words, are at the root of everything we experience in life, which is why consciously choosing what rolls around in your mind and falls out of your mouth is one of the most important things you can do. This conscious choosing of your thoughts, beliefs, and words is called mastering your mindset, and master it you must if you'd like to live large and in charge.

If you want more success, money, and happiness, then it's crucial that you stop believing money myths and master your mindset about money.

Let's look at some of the common myths we've believed about money.

MYTH #1: Money Is Evil

We've all heard it said that money is the root of all evil. Maybe your parents reinforced this myth when you were growing up. Many people have attributed the phrase to the Bible, but this isn't true.

The Apostle Paul once wrote a letter to Timothy that said, "The love of money is the root of all evil." ***That is not the same thing!***

What Paul was talking about is **greed**, the desire to collect and hoard wealth simply because you can, and the willingness to do whatever it takes to obtain that fortune.

After all, money itself is just an inanimate object. It's a piece of paper, a chunk of metal like a gold bar, or some digital numbers in your bank account. Is that paper or metal inherently evil?

Nope! Money itself is neutral. It's not good, and it's not bad.

Think about it this way. When you put a $20 bill in your wallet, does that make you a worse person?

Of course not. What if you put a $100 bill in your wallet?

You're still not a bad person.

Adding more money to your bank account doesn't mean that you're somehow adding something bad to your life. You're simply adding more numbers to your account.

Here's the key point: ***It's how you obtain the money and what you***

do with it, not the money itself, that is good or bad.

When Paul wrote about the love of money being the root of all evil, ***he was talking about the immoral ways people obtain it.*** We can all see it would be wrong to murder people for money or to rob people at gunpoint. But he was also talking about making a larger profit directly at the expense of others.

But that isn't the same thing as starting your own business, providing a new service, or investing your money in a new venture.

And with this new capital, you can do great things with money!

- You can give it to people in need.
- You can buy something for yourself that you really want.
- You can start a charity.
- You can help your friend start a business.

You get the point. It's the actions you take, not money itself, that is evil.

MYTH #2: People Who Want Money Are Greedy

Many of us carry around the assumption that only people who are greedy want more money. We assume that if we want money, we'll become like Ebenezer Scrooge, always hoarding money but never giving it away.

But is this true?

No.

Again, money is a neutral thing. It's what you do with the money that truly matters. 20 CREATE YOUR MILLIONAIRE MINDSET So yes, you can be greedy and simply want to accumulate as much money as possible. But having more money also allows you to be extremely generous. It allows you to give good things to others. It allows you to donate to charity. Since becoming a Christian, I have given a percentage of my income to charity every year. Guess what? I haven't missed it and the feeling of helping others is amazing! You simply can't do those things if you don't have money.

Did you catch that?

You can't be generous if you don't have money.

Think about that for a minute.

If you want to be financially generous, you have to have some finances in the first place.

It's time to kill this myth. Wanting more money does not make you greedy.

MYTH #3: There Is Not Enough Money

If you grew up in a house where finances were regularly "tight," then you may harbor the belief that there simply isn't enough money to go around. As I shared earlier, I grew up in a family that didn't have a lot of money. On top of that, my dad got hurt at work and the resulting medical bills and career change left a financial impact that followed us for years. As a result, this is an area I struggle with. But let's step back a minute and evaluate this belief.

How much money is in the world?

Trillions and trillions of dollars.

There is more than enough money for everyone. There is no scarcity of money. In fact, there is an actual abundance of money in the world. Just because you don't have all the money that you want doesn't mean that there's not enough.

This is the difference between a "scarcity" mindset and an "abundance" mindset:

- *With a scarcity mindset, you believe that there is never enough.* You feel like you have to hold onto everything you have because you never know when it will be gone.

- *With an abundance mindset, you believe that there is more than enough for everyone.* You realize that when you get money, it doesn't mean that someone else is not getting money.

Money is not a zero-sum game. In other words, you receiving money does not mean that someone else is losing money.

That's just not how it works.

There's plenty for everyone. We live in a world of abundance.

MYTH #4: I'll Never Make Enough Money

You miss 100% of the shots you don't take, so if you believe you will never make enough money, you are only going to prove yourself right. It's a self-fulfilling prophecy.

But why do you have that belief in the first place?

If there is more than enough money in the world for everyone, why should you believe that you'll never make enough?

You're an incredibly talented person that has so much to offer the world, and it's critical that you believe that. Your skills, talents, and expertise are worth money, and there are lots of people out there who are willing to pay for those skills.

But in order for this to be your reality, you have to believe it first.

You have to stop buying into the lie that you'll never make enough money and start affirming that you are going to make more than you can imagine.

You may not know exactly how you're going to make the money, but that's okay. You have to master your mindset, and that means having the unshakeable belief that you're going to increase your income.

You can and will make more than enough money if you're willing to believe it first.

MYTH #5: If I Make More Money, People Won't Like Me

This is a common myth that many people believe, especially if their parents didn't like people who had money.

But the reality is we don't dislike people who make money. We dislike people who flaunt their wealth in an arrogant way.

Again, this goes back to how you use your money. If you make more money and then start bragging to your friends about how awesome you are, then sure, they might not like you anymore.

But if you use your increased income to help others, people will actually like you more! And they certainly won't begrudge you for spending some on yourself.

As long as you don't flaunt your wealth in an annoying, arrogant way, you'll be just fine. In fact, people will probably appreciate you more as you accumulate wealth.

MYTH #6: I'm Just Fine Without Money

Money may not be able to buy happiness, but it sure doesn't hurt. If you've struggled for a long time to achieve financial stability, then you may have convinced yourself that you're just fine without having any money.

But is this really true?

- Are you really living your absolute best life?

- Are you the best version of yourself that you can be?

- Are you able to live fearlessly, generously, and joyfully?

- Do you feel safe spending money, or do you live in anticipation of the next unexpected expense?

Let's be honest: money makes many things possible that aren't possible otherwise.

Money allows you to expand your horizons by traveling the world. It allows you to deepen friendships by going out to dinner with your close friends. It allows you to support worthy causes. It can give you peace of mind in an uncertain future by providing a safety net.

If you don't have money, you can't expand into your full potential. ***You can't be your best self.***

To be clear, I'm not saying that people without money are somehow defective. I'm simply saying that money gives you options that you wouldn't have otherwise.

Let's be done with this myth. ***It's time for you to achieve your true greatness.***

"Beliefs have the power to create and the power to destroy. Human beings have the awesome ability to take any experience of their lives and create a meaning that disempowers them or one that can literally save their lives."

- Tony Robbins

#3

Are Limiting Beliefs Holding You Back?

Your brain is the most important organ in your body. It is a mean, lean, complex information processing machine, and it's considered by experts to be the most powerful computer in the world. It uses over 100 billion neurons to send information through the body at well over 150 miles per hour, a process that generates enough power to light up a light bulb. (Yes, for real!)

The complexity of the human mind is what has allowed us to become the dominant species on the planet, but it is also the reason you may carry around some incorrect beliefs.

You see, human beings learn and store information as patterns. We build on our previous knowledge, similar to a bricklayer building a new wall. Each row of bricks is built on top of the previous row, just like our new beliefs and thoughts are built on the knowledge we had before. This allows us to make better and faster decisions, which helps us adapt and survive in any environment.

The problem is sometimes people learn the wrong thing or apply correct information in the wrong scenario, which can lead to a lot of other false conclusions. *These false conclusions can turn into*

limiting beliefs.

What is a limiting belief? For our purposes, here's a definition:

"A limiting belief is one that causes life to be less than completely satisfying"

In other words, ***they are self-imposed limits that stop you from reaching your full potential.*** We all carry around numerous limiting beliefs. They tell us we aren't good enough, not strong enough, or not smart enough to accomplish our dreams. Limiting beliefs come from a variety of sources as well as from our own interpretation of the world around us. As we said before, humans sometimes learn the wrong lesson from their observations.

For example, I didn't have friends in school. I got picked on and teased, and this has led me to a wrong belief that people don't want to be my friend. I have spent much of my life not building and nurturing friendships because of this belief. When I share this with people, they tell me I'm wrong, they do appreciate me and want to be my friend. Fortunately, we can unlearn these limiting beliefs and replace them with beliefs that empower us.

It's important to follow a plan or process. Most things in life are like baking a cake. If you do all the right things in the right order, you'll get a cake in the end. It's impossible to have any other result. Likewise, by following a process, you can banish your limiting beliefs.

If you doubt that you have any limiting beliefs, consider this: If all your beliefs are 100% accurate, you should have been able to achieve and earn everything you've ever wanted. Is this true for you?

If there is even one area in your life that you are not satisfied with, you should open up your mind and consider the possibility that you were taught the wrong lesson at some point. What do you have to lose?

> ***"Old beliefs die hard even when demonstrably false."***

> **— E. O. Wilson**

How Limiting Beliefs Affect Your Life

There is no shortage of advice out there about how to achieve your dreams. Some people say you need to write them down, while others insist there needs to be a deadline. The specifics may differ, but they all basically follow the same steps. In this book, we are going to remember these steps with the acronym DARE.

Decide	It's tough to accomplish something meaningful if you don't identify it first. You must decide clearly what you want before you can do anything.
Act	It takes action to attain any goal. Some people claim that you can practically wish a Porsche into your driveway without lifting a finger, but the real truth is that some action is required. You'll have to do something to accomplish anything meaningful.
Revise	You might not know enough at first to realize the perfect path. Adjust your approach as you gain new expertise. If it's not working, don't be afraid to try something else.
Endure	If you kept improving your approach and you never gave up, how could you possibly fail? We spend too much time figuring out ways to work around our faulty beliefs. Once you find an approach that works, ***you just need to keep going until you're successful.***

In this process, every step is a little harder than the last. We all have dreams, so clarifying exactly what we want is fairly easy. Step two is a little harder, and it is the most common place to be tripped up by a limiting belief. As was stated earlier, most people won't take an action they think is doomed to fail. We think to ourselves: "Why should I bother?" ***This is exactly how limiting beliefs get in our way.***

Another way limiting beliefs can impede your progress is by

convincing you there is only one way to succeed. Once they get started, some people are afraid to stray from the plan they made in step one. **This is a mistake!** There is no shame in adapting your plan after you gain more experience. Being flexible allows you to roll with the punches and increases your chance of success.

The last step is the most difficult step in this process, and many people are unable to complete it. Most of us decide too quickly that something won't work. As soon as you believe it won't work, you're unlikely to continue working towards your goal.

Let's look at an example. Stephen King is one of the best-selling authors of all time, having sold over 400 million books as of 2022. He has written more than 200 short stories and at least 64 novels under a variety of pen names. His works include *Pet Cemetery, The Shining, Gerald's Game*, and the clown-centric horror classic *It*.

But success did not come easily to Mr. King. His very first novel was rejected by more than 30 publishers, all of whom repeatedly told him that it would never sell. Fortunately, Stephen King kept trying until he finally found a small publishing house that saw merit in his story. Together they published his debut novel *Carrie*, which has sold over 66 million copies worldwide and has been adapted into film four separate times.

Achieving big things usually requires time and effort. Most of the time, that requires an intelligent and calculated effort, as opposed to stubborn determination. It takes time and experience to put forth the most effective strategy, but you won't be able to get there with a limiting belief in the way.

Besides preventing your success, limiting beliefs also negatively affect your life in other ways, such as:

1. **You'll be inefficient.** Limiting beliefs cause us to find an alternate path if we bother to look for one at all. They are like obstacles we put in our own way, which means we spend a lot of unnecessary time and effort trying to go around them. Save some time and deal with the limiting belief instead.

2. **You unintentionally harm those around you.** Even with the best intentions, you affect others with your limiting beliefs. You'll likely teach your children false ideas that limit them and even affect your friends with misinformed advice.

3. **You will live a less fulfilling life.** You will do fewer things over the course of your life when you're constricted by your limiting beliefs. Imagine what your life would be like without any limiting beliefs. Surely a fuller, richer life is more appealing to you, no matter how great your life is right now.

4. **You fail to grow fully as a human being.** It can be useful to view life with the purpose of eliminating your limiting beliefs and experiencing everything in the world that appeals to you. When you self-reflect and eliminate limiting beliefs, you are most likely ridding yourself of internalized prejudices and

outdated ideas. By doing so, you are not only making the world a better and more welcoming place, but you are also making yourself a better person. Opening yourself up to new ideas and experiences can completely change the trajectory of your life for the better.

Are you ready to DARE yourself to live a better life?

> ***"If you don't change your beliefs, your life will be like this forever. Is that good news?"***
>
> **—W. Somerset Maugham**

How Can You Tell if a Limiting Belief Is False?

Obviously, there are some things that are genuinely impossible. No matter how hard you try and how strongly you believe, you won't ever be able to run faster than the speed of light. So, some limiting beliefs are accurate, and it would be silly to argue otherwise.

However, most of our limiting beliefs are inaccurate.

A limiting belief could be false if:

- **It is not 100% true in every situation.** If your belief isn't true all the time in different situations and it doesn't seem to be true for other people in the way it seems true for you, it might be false.
- **It's not based on experience.** If your belief isn't based

on actual personal experience, it might be false. To a large extent, you don't know what you can and can't do until you try. Many times, you might need to make 100 attempts or more to know the truth.

- **It's not based on a real physical limitation.** If your belief isn't based on a real physical limitation, it might be false. For example, it might seem logical to say you can't fly because you will never be able to flap your arms and lift off the ground like a bird. However, there is nothing stopping you from going to flight school and becoming a pilot.

It ignores the opinion of experts. If your belief isn't based on the opinion of experts, it might be false. It's important to fact-check, but you don't need to reinvent the wheel here. For example, most of us have never seen a Great White Shark in real life, but that doesn't mean they don't exist. If your experience contradicts expert opinion and large amounts of evidence, you should reflect on why that is. What is different about your experience that could have changed the results?

> *"Beliefs don't change facts. Facts, if you're reasonable, should change your beliefs."*
>
> **—Ricky Gervais**

How Do You Acquire a Limiting Belief?

Limiting beliefs are pervasive in our lives, and they come from a variety of sources. Some of these sources might surprise you. Most of the time, they came from people who were actually trying to help us. So don't blame them, they simply believed the wrong things too.

The most common source of limiting beliefs is our family. They have known us since we were young and suggestible, and as a result their words often leave a bigger impact than we realize. For example, maybe your mom told you in high school you were too heavy to run track. As a result of that comment, you may now believe you could never be a runner. Another example is if no one in your family has ever gone to college, you may believe that higher education isn't a possibility for you.

Much like our families, friends can say and do things that lead us to believe we're less capable than we really are. Since we usually trust our friends, we are more likely to take their words to heart and believe them. ***It's important to remember that other people tend to unintentionally push their limiting beliefs on others.*** You should also keep in mind that some of our 'friends' don't want to see others do better than they themselves are doing.

Teachers are another common source of limiting beliefs, as they can have a lot of influence over our formative years. It is their job to educate and prepare us for the real world. It's entirely possible that they may have accidentally passed on some of their own limiting beliefs in the process. After all, teachers are people too! Some of them have their stuff together, some do not.

An example of this would be if your 1st-grade teacher told you that you would never be a good reader. As a result, you may believe that reading just isn't for you. And if you identify as someone who hates reading, you will almost certainly miss the opportunity to read books that would have changed your life!

Another major source of limiting beliefs is ***yourself***. Specifically, the way you interpret events in your life. In many ways, this is probably the only real source of our limiting beliefs. For instance, if your parents repeatedly said, "You can't get into college if you don't have good grades," they were likely trying to encourage you to do your very best in school. But if you interpreted that statement as "Your grades aren't good enough to get you into college," then you may feel like college isn't an option for you, leading you to actually put *less* effort into school.

In this instance, it's not really what your parents said to you, it's how you interpreted what was said that matters. ***Limiting beliefs are born when you decide to believe your own interpretation of others' comments.***

My experience of being picked on in school, not fitting in with the 'cool kids', and not having many friends growing up has caused me to have a number of limiting beliefs such as I'm not likable, people will reject me, I'm not good enough, and many more.

These can be hard to shake because our RAS (reticular activating system) looks for evidence to support our beliefs and solidify them as true. So, in my example here, when a prospective client decides not to work with me, it can be interpreted internally as support for "See I'm not likable, this is another proof point."

These are just a few examples of the most common sources. Strangers, the internet, advertisements, movies, the news, coworkers, and more all have the opportunity to give us pause and doubt. Consider all the sources of information and opinion in your life. Every single one of them has the opportunity to steer you in the wrong direction.

As Elenor Roosevelt once said, "No one can make you feel inferior without your consent." It doesn't matter what other people think you can and can't do. ***All that matters is what YOU believe you can do.***

Discovering Your Limiting Beliefs

As we talked about earlier, a big part of being successful is knowing how to use your time and energy effectively. We all have tons of limiting beliefs, but the truth is that many of them are irrelevant. So, for now, only worry about the limiting beliefs that are going to have the greatest impact. Once you've dealt with those, then you can deal with the others.

Before you can change anything, you first have to identify the problem. Let's go through the process of discovering your limiting beliefs.

IDENTIFYING YOUR LIMITING BELIEFS

Step 1. Make a list of the areas in your life where you feel challenged. If you have an area of your life that displeases you and you're not actively doing something to fix it, then it's a pretty good bet that you have a limiting belief. Otherwise, you would already be working to fix the situation. Life is a mirror, and your behavior is an indicator of your beliefs.

Consider how you're doing in the following areas:

•**Finances.** Are you feeling financial pressure in your life? Do you have all the things you need or really want? How much money do you have in your savings? Do you have the income you desire? Is that income secure?

- **Relationships.** Are your relationships satisfying? Consider your relationships with your family, friends, and co-workers in addition to your intimate relationship with your significant other. How do your loved ones support you? How do you support them? How does spending time with these people make you feel about yourself?

- **Health.** Are you taking good care of yourself? Are you happy with the way you look? Do you go to the doctor regularly for checkups? Are you eating healthy food regularly? Don't forget to think about your mental health. What have your stress levels been like recently?

- **Fun and Adventure.** Have you been making time for the things you really want to do? Do you dream of going to Europe but haven't been? Do you want to learn to play the piano but never have? Have you always wanted to learn a new language but never found the time?

- **Think about any other areas of your life where you're less than thrilled.** If you're not pleased with your life, a limiting belief could be the cause.

Step 2. Identify the beliefs that are contributing to your challenges. Make a list of all your beliefs, good and bad, regarding the challenges you identified above. Don't attempt to filter them as positive or negative while doing this process; just get them all listed as you brainstorm and examine them later.

Here's a short example around money:

- Making over $100k a year is really hard.

- Life is too hard for me to be wealthy.

- Rich people are dishonest.

- I'll never have enough money to travel the world.

- If I'm rich, people will try to steal from me.

- My friends will treat me differently if I have a lot of money.

Can you see how all these beliefs would make it difficult for you to make a lot of money?

Step 3. Identify the beliefs that are holding you back.

Look at the list you have brainstormed. Think about which of these beliefs is having the greatest negative impact on your life. One way to do this is to consider how your behavior would change if that belief were eliminated from your life.

Don't just guess which beliefs are the most damaging. Really examine it and consider the change that your life would experience if you weren't held back by that belief.

Step 4. Put those negative beliefs in order.

Start with the limiting belief that you feel is creating the most challenge in your life. Put them all in order from the belief having the greatest negative impact to the least impact. Prioritizing your time is always a valuable strategy, and it makes sense to spend your time where it's going to do the most good.

Now that you have a list of your limiting beliefs and have them in order, it's time to start dealing with them.

"If you develop the absolute sense of certainty that powerful beliefs provide, then you can get yourself to accomplish virtually anything, including those things that other people are certain are impossible."

—William Lyon Phelps

How to Eliminate a Limiting Belief

Follow this 7-step process to banish a limiting belief:

Step 1. Read the belief aloud and ask yourself, "Do I really know that this is true?"

- Have you experienced this yourself enough times to be confident that it is true? Remember: you can't accurately draw conclusions from a limited number of experiences.

- Do you really know that this belief is true without a shred of doubt?

Step 2. Where did you come up with this belief?

- For example, did your limiting belief about money come from your mom? Was your mom a wealthy person? If she wasn't at that time, then she's not a reliable source of information. After all, an expert on money would be able to have a lot of it. And someone who hasn't had a lot of money is unlikely to know how to accumulate it or what it means to have it. Consider whether or not the source of your beliefs is a valid source.

• Your beliefs should come from your own personal experiences and from the advice of experts. That's it. If your dad wasn't a great college student, you can find a better source of information about what it takes to be successful in college.

• **Rely on experts.** They are easy to find with a little research. If you can't find an expert that supports your belief, it is probably false.

Step 3. Simply state to yourself, "I choose not to believe this anymore.

It's not true."

• It might sound trite, but stating your intention has a profound effect.

• Look for supporting evidence from trustworthy sources. Find some reasons and examples why this limiting belief is false. For example:

– The person that told me this doesn't really know.

– I've never actually tried it for myself.

– I've seen others that are less capable than me be successful at this.

- If you do this with an open mind, you should feel a sense of doubt about that limiting belief. If you don't, then keep coming up with more reasons. Get online and read some articles by someone that you feel is truly an expert on the topic of your belief. Search for examples that the belief is false.

Step 4. Create a new belief that serves you.

- This will likely be the opposite of the limiting belief or at least something along those lines. Create a belief that will empower you and help make your life better.

- Find examples to support this new belief. Any belief will be more stable if it has supporting information and evidence.

- Really work to prove that it's true. Imagine you are back in high school, and you are going to have to give a presentation on why your new belief is accurate. That should get you where you need to be.

Step 5. Measure yourself.

- Each day, check yourself. How do you feel about your new belief? How do you feel about your old belief? Listen to your gut; it's a direct link to your subconscious.

- Is your behavior changing? Our actions and feelings are a manifestation of our beliefs. If your beliefs have really changed, your life will change as well.

Step 6. Go back to your list of limiting beliefs.

- Keep working on your list of negative beliefs. Work through those items and continue to add new items to it. You'll find that you'll discover new limiting beliefs as you start making progress in your life.

- As you experience new things, new limiting beliefs will show up. These are beliefs that you didn't know you had until this point.

- As you set new goals, new challenges will present themselves. As you learn and experience more, your objectives change, so the limiting beliefs you have will change, too. Maybe you'll decide 10 years from now that you want to be a doctor; any limiting beliefs you have about becoming a doctor would then have to be addressed.

- Continue examining your life for limiting beliefs and eliminating them. It's like pulling weeds. No matter what you do, some weeds always pop up over time. Simply recognize them and get rid of them.

Step 7. Repeat all the steps on a regular basis.

- As you set a new goal or have new challenges in your life, repeat the process. It would be a great idea to sit down and make a new list of limiting beliefs once a week. You would be unstoppable.

"Sometimes all it takes to change a life is to decide which beliefs do not serve you and to literally change your mind about those beliefs."

- Joy Page

Summary

Limiting beliefs really do put our lives in a stranglehold. They can lead us to believe that we have limited options to deal with our challenges or that we're limited in doing new things. These beliefs have profound negative consequences and eliminating them is one of the best things we can do for ourselves.

Our limiting beliefs come from a variety of sources: friends, family, teachers, neighbors, the media, and our own interpretation of the world and the events in our lives. In many cases, the source of the limiting belief truly had our best interests at heart. That doesn't change the fact that they may have passed untrue beliefs on to you.

By examining those beliefs and asking ourselves some key questions, we can eliminate them. Unless we've experienced something numerous times or we have the advice of an expert, we don't really have the knowledge to make accurate judgments about something. Be selective about who you believe.

Once you have singled out a limiting belief that you need to eliminate, you will have to replace it with a new empowering belief. A new belief needs evidence to support it before it can be believed. You will see the way this new belief is changing your life in the form of new behaviors and different results.

One of the limiting beliefs I shared earlier about myself is "I'm not likable" and this has held me back for years from having meaningful friendships.

I have done the work to know this is not true. So now when that comes up in my mind, I replace it with "I'm lovable and many people have told me so".

This is why the measurement process is so critical; it's important to see if the new belief is in place and if it is indeed an empowering belief.

By systematically going through all of your limiting beliefs, it's possible to dramatically improve your life. Always remember that new limiting beliefs will occur over time, and it's important to check yourself regularly for these new limiting beliefs.

Once you deal with your mental obstacles, you'll soon see those are the biggest obstacles you have.

Look at your limiting beliefs today – your life will never be the same!

What limiting beliefs come into your mind that would be helpful to jot down?

"In order to carry a positive action we must develop a positive vision."

- *Tony Robbins*

#4

The Power Of Your Mind: Having An Abundance Mindset

What you think about has an incredible effect on the quality of your life and whether you reach your dreams. Every outcome you're experiencing right now, whether it's positive or negative, is primarily the result of your thoughts.

Your focus determines what you attract:

- Focus on positive things, and you'll attract positive things.

- Focus on negative things, and you'll attract the negative.

If this sounds familiar, it's probably because this isn't a new idea. People have been using this mindset to attain success since the second century! In fact, the Roman Emperor and philosopher Marcus Aurelius once said:

The happiness of your life depends upon the quality of your thoughts. Therefore, guard accordingly, and take care that you entertain no notions unsuitable to virtue and reasonable nature.

This is true. ***The happiness of your life and the reality you create depends primarily upon your thoughts. That's how powerful your brain is.***

The massive implication here is if you're not experiencing what you want in your **outer world** (reality), it's likely due to what's happening in your **inner world** (your thoughts, desires, and dreams). Remember that life is a mirror, your outer world is just a reflection of what your inner world is attracting.

- Not attracting the wealth you want? Inner world.

- Not able to get your head above water financially? Inner world.

- Not able to move forward in your job as you should? Inner world.

T. Harv Ecker puts it like this:

> ***Whatever results you're getting, be they rich or poor, good or bad, positive or negative, always remember that your outer world is simply a reflection of your inner world. If things aren't going well in your outer life, it's because things aren't going well in your inner life. It's that simple.***

The good news is that *you are the one in control of your inner world.* You determine what you think about and focus on. The more you control and shape your inner world, the more you will control and shape your actual reality.

This means if you want to change your life and attract more wealth, you absolutely must master the way you think. *You must adopt a mindset of abundance, gratitude, and positivity.*

The Power of Abundance

An abundance mindset is hopeful, positive, and expects the best. It is also more altruistic since you believe that you'll receive what you need. It frees you up to do more for others.

On the other hand, a scarcity mindset leads to negativity and selfishness. You feel the need to look out for yourself, even at the expense of others.

Viewing the world from a position of abundance versus one of scarcity has various positive effects on your life:

1.   **An abundance mindset believes that there is plenty to go around.** You believe there is plenty of money in the world, plenty of potential partners, and plenty of opportunities in general.

   −A scarcity mindset believes there is a limited supply of everything, and *that someone else must lose in order for you to win.*

2.   Life is easier with an abundance mindset. You believe that anything is possible. With that attitude, you're willing to try and you expect things will eventually go your way.

–If you have a scarcity mindset, you believe that life is difficult. You see success as being harder than it really is. You expect the worst and might convince yourself that it's pointless to even try. ***It's much more challenging to be successful with a scarcity mindset.***

3.   Opportunities are easier to see when you expect to find them. Seek and ye shall find! An abundance mindset makes opportunities more visible.

–If you believe opportunities are scarce, you'll struggle to find them. This is true even if they're right in front of your face.

4.   You take more risks with an abundance mindset. You believe the likelihood of success is greater, so you take more risks. The more you risk, the more you stand to gain. You also potentially have more to lose, but that's part of the game. ***Those who are bold tend to outperform those who are timid.***

–You're more likely to play it safe if you view the world from a position of scarcity. ***You're more afraid of losing what you have since you believe it will be difficult to get it back.***

5. Those with an abundance mindset are more relaxed. When you believe the world has everything you need, you can relax and enjoy life.

You view the possibilities as endless, and your overall viewpoint of life is more positive.

–A scarcity mindset results in fear and pessimism. You believe you have to fight the world to get what you want and need. You have to protect what you have from loss.

Do you think your view of the world is one of abundance or scarcity? If you hold a scarcity mindset, it's worth trying another viewpoint on for size.

One of the best ways to start viewing the world with abundance is to give more. You can give money, your time, or give away a few of your possessions. Giving will enforce the idea that there is always enough to go around.

Abundance will flow into your life if you allow it. After holding an abundance mindset for a few months, contrast that with your previous experience with scarcity. Choose the one that works for you.

Changing Your Mind About Money

We talked about limiting beliefs and how they affect your life in the last chapter. But now that we know your outer world is a reflection of your inner world, shedding these beliefs and embracing an abundance mindset is even more important.

What you believe becomes your reality.

Therefore, it's important to believe:

- There's enough money for everyone.

- You are capable of receiving it.

- You simply need to reach out and take it.

Whether you believe in God, universal intelligence, or the energy behind all things, you must believe that it wants you to succeed. Because it really does, and by thinking otherwise, you are sabotaging yourself before you even begin.

The world is full of abundance! That means if you're living in scarcity, you're not enjoying all the world has to offer.

It's time to change your mind about money. To believe that there's enough, that you deserve to have money, you are capable of receiving it, and that you were created to experience abundance.

Regularly affirm this. Tell yourself these things over and over again until they're burned into your brain. Until you believe them with all your heart and soul.

Only then will you be ready to accept the opportunities that come your way.

Opportunities Are Everywhere

Once you start having an abundance mindset and open yourself up to all that the Creator wants to give you, you'll start seeing opportunities everywhere.

- You'll think of new ways to acquire money that you would never have considered before.

- Opportunities will drop into your lap out of nowhere.

- You'll begin to attract money in ways that surprise you.

But first, you must open your mind to the possibilities that are all around you. The world is full of infinite possibilities; just because you can't see them doesn't mean they aren't there.

Recently I've had nine months in a row of our best month ever. Things just seemed to come out of nowhere. Folks would tell me they found out about us from a Google search, from a friend, or even that they've been getting our emails or LinkedIn messages for over a year and want to chat. When I simply trust that the opportunities will come, they do. It is important for me to have a daily routine, otherwise I tend to fall in and out of this belief.

Angelina Zimmerman puts it this way:

The scarcity pathway leads one to experience a life not fully lived, a life that can only be described as pedestrian.

Overflowing with strong negative reactions like the high tide that creates waves in a rock pool not to mention the countless missed opportunities and experiences.

Those that choose to walk along the path of abundance experience a completely different life. Opting to live life to the full, exuding happiness, generous by nature, creative and inspirational. Taking full advantage and enjoying the wave of opportunities that come their way, along with memorable experiences.

One of the best ways to choose abundance is through the practice of gratitude.

Start practicing gratitude for all the things you currently have and all the ways your needs are currently being met. When you receive something good and positive, say a simple "Thank you." This practice will start to transform the way you live.

It doesn't matter if you are thanking God, the Creator, fate, or the universe as a whole. When you're grateful for even the smallest things, it puts positive energy out into the world, which then attracts more positive things into your life.

It really is a powerful cycle. You put out the positive energy of gratitude, and you are rewarded with more things to be grateful for.

Taking Action On Your Dreams

An abundance mindset is absolutely necessary if you want to attract wealth and build your dreams. ***But an abundance mindset alone is not enough.***

ACTION is needed.

In other words, you may have an abundance mindset, but if you don't start taking action on your dreams, nothing will change. However, an abundance mindset combined with action leads to great things.

THE EQUATION OF SUCCESS IS:

Abundance + Action = Dreams Become Reality

Once you start taking action, you'll begin to see the things you dreamed about becoming an actual reality. ***You will achieve more than you thought possible.*** There is absolutely nothing that can stop you.

Isn't that exciting to think about? Doesn't that get you fired up?

When taking action on your dreams, follow these steps…

Step #1: Write Your Dreams Down

The first step is to write down your dreams and goals. You will want to be as specific as possible. You want to be able to see every detail in your mind's eye.

Ask yourself questions like:

- What do I want to get out of life?

- What are my biggest dreams?

- What do I want to accomplish?

- How much money do I want to make?

- When do I want to make it by?

The more detailed you can be when writing down your dreams and goals, the more you'll be able to visualize them coming true. The more you can visualize them, the better you will feel about them. The better you feel about your goals, the more focused you will be. Finally, the more focused you are on your dreams, the more you'll attract them into your life.

It's really that simple.

T. Harv Ecker calls this **the wealth principle:**

WEALTH PRINCIPLE:

Thoughts lead to feelings. Feelings lead to actions. Actions lead to results.

So, ***think*** about your dreams and goals, and write them down in as much detail as possible. Then reflect on your dreams intensely. ***Feel*** how amazing it will be when you accomplish them. As you feel this passion, allow it to motivate you to ***action***, which will then translate into absolutely amazing results.

Step #2: Affirm Your Dreams Daily

After you've written down your goals, it's important that you start rehearsing them *as you start to take action.* It is important to do this as you are taking action because you need both to succeed. Action without affirmation leads to burnout and discouragement. Affirmation without action leads to stalling and wasted opportunities. *You cannot have one without the other.*

Repeat your dreams to yourself every single day. Affirm that they are going to come true.

Say things like:

- "I affirm that I am going to double my income by XX date."

- "I affirm that I am becoming a financial success in all areas of my life."

- "I affirm that I will break the company sales record this year."

- "I affirm that this will be my best year ever financially."

Repeat these affirmations again and again until you believe with all your heart that they're true. Even if you don't know how these things are going to happen, affirm that they will. These kinds of affirmations create positive energy around you that will keep you motivated and on track.

The energy that you put out into the world has a way of coming back to you. If you put out positive energy in the form of affirmations and gratitude, you'll see that positive energy return to you in positive forms.

Step #3: Start Taking Action on Your Dreams

Once you've written down your dreams and begun to rehearse them each day, it's crucial to start taking action.

Map out what specific steps you need to follow in order to achieve your dreams, and then begin taking those actions.

What do you need to do to make your dreams a reality? Don't worry if you don't have this all figured out. Just brainstorm and begin taking action on whatever comes to mind.

- Hire a mentor

- Call an expert who can give you advice or guidance

- Start building another business on the side

- Call a friend you haven't spoken to in a while

- Start doing research on laws that may apply to your dream

- Send an email to an important contact

- Get some price estimates on supplies and equipment you may need to get started

If you have an abundance mindset and are open to new

opportunities, actions will begin to pop into your mind. You'll start to have ideas that you didn't have before.

Take action on these ideas. These are cues that are intended to guide you on the path to wealth and success.

Make it your goal to take at least one action on your dreams every single day. Even something small, like sending an email, doing some research, or making a list will move you at least a little bit closer to achieving what you truly want.

Over two years ago, I was introduced to the idea of a mindset coach, and I took action by hiring my Mindset Coach to help me on this journey. As part of that journey, I created a mind movie that represents my dreams that I watch each morning. I also started a podcast about a year ago, and instead of overthinking it and overplanning, I just started and have learned along the way. That podcast has brought us clients that we would not have otherwise met.

The more you take action, the more impressive the results you'll see. You'll achieve things you never believed were possible and you'll realize that you truly do have limitless potential.

As Gary John Bishop says:

> *...the person who views success as if it were just around the corner will not only work his butt off to achieve it but be energized and alive to it all the while acting on that fundamental view of success... You see, our thoughts are so powerful that they are constantly pushing you toward your goals, even when you don't realize what those goals actually are! Your brain is wired to win.*

Your Dreams Are Waiting for You

And now for the million-dollar question: What are you going to do with your life?

You now know that:

- You truly have limitless potential.

- Most of the myths you've believed about money are totally false.

- Your inner thoughts control your outer reality.

- You have the power to shape your reality.

- You can attract and manifest the wealth and dreams that you desire.

- The Creator totally has your back and is supporting your dreams.

Are you going to take control of your destiny, master your money mindset, and achieve your dreams? Or are you going to continue struggling?

There is an amazing future out there, just waiting for you to seize it. Don't let that future pass you by.

Master your money mindset today and watch what begins to happen. You'll be absolutely floored by the results!

"Never underestimate the power of dreams and the influence of the human spirit. We are all the same in this notion: The potential for greatness lives within each of us."

- Wilma Rudolph

#5

Moving Forward

At the beginning of this book, I asked you to keep an open mind and give some new ideas a chance. Do these new ideas still sound crazy? Do you understand the effect a good mindset can have on your life?

If you have been feeling financially stuck or asleep at the wheel, it is time for you to try something new. After all, what do you have to lose?

It's time to change your mindset.

It's time to fulfill your potential.

You have already taken the first step in your financial journey by picking up and reading this book. The next step is answering the questions listed after this chapter. But if you are having trouble figuring out what to do after that, let's review the most important things you can do for yourself on this financial journey.

Question What You Believe Is Possible

No matter how independent you are, everyone is influenced by the people around them. That's why identifying and eliminating limiting beliefs isn't just the first step of your journey to financial success; It's a step you need to revisit periodically as you grow. If you are feeling discouraged or feel like you have hit a dead end, *it may be time to reflect on what you believe to be fact.* You may have picked up a limiting belief that is stopping you from seeing a new opportunity. Remember:

- Money is not inherently evil.

- Wanting more money doesn't make you greedy.

- There is enough money to go around.

- You are capable of earning more money and making your life easier.

Study the Actions of Successful People

Marian Wright Edelman once famously said, "You can't be what you can't see." It's not impossible to succeed without a role model to look up to but following in someone else's footsteps is easier than blazing your own trail.

In other words, it's always easier when we have an example to follow. Work smarter, not harder. *Learn by example.*

Find someone successful whom you admire and do what they do. These individuals serve as proof that your dreams can come true.

- Find someone who has had the same kind of success that you desire.

- Study what they've done right as well as their mistakes.

By studying what they did to reach success, you will not only learn from their tactics and avoid repeating their failures, but you will also be reminded that your dreams are possible. ***That's why this is possibly the most important advice on this list.***

Find a way to ask successful people questions. You might be surprised to know that successful people love to inspire others to find success as well. They know that there's plenty of success to go around. That's the prosperity mindset in action!

It's All About Being Positive

If you believe in yourself, you can achieve your dreams. You become a self-fulfilling prophecy the moment you think you can't do something. We know that negative feelings arise from time to time, and that's okay. However, you need to keep a positive image of the big picture in your mind at all times. Keeping an abundance mindset will not only help you avoid internalizing limiting beliefs, but it will also help you see the world and opportunities in a new way.

- Picture yourself reaching your goals and imagine how it feels.

- Surround yourself with positive people.

- Be generous when you can.

- Write prosperity affirmations.

- Be an open person.

- Be grateful for what you have.

When you open up to new opportunities, you open up to prosperity. Stay motivated and don't be afraid of change.

Setting Goals and Action Plans

You can dream all day about where you'd like your life to go, but nothing will happen without a goal or an action plan. Take time to think about the big picture and then start to map out how you're going to get there.

Write out your goals and be as specific as possible. Physically writing them down will help them feel more real and help you effectively brainstorm. This will help you visualize and focus on your dreams, which will help you attract them into your life.

- Break down your goals into smaller steps.

- Set manageable and achievable goals.

- Adapt your plan as you learn and grow but hold yourself accountable.

Don't Give Up

You need to have the dedicated motivation and drive to tell yourself that you'll stop at nothing before you reach success. When you talk to or study the actions of someone who is successful, they'll likely tell you tales of their many failures. There were probably times when they felt like giving up, but they were able to push through defeat.

Regular affirmations will help you get through moments when you feel discouraged or burnt out. Affirmations will also help you maintain a positive mindset, which will help you attract more positive things into your life.

•Realize that everyone feels like giving up, but we can't give in to these feelings.

- Keep the image of your goal in your mind.

- Make changes if you need to but continue taking action toward your goal.

Get a Coach

Prosperity mindsets can look different from person to person. They have different approaches to getting what they want, and different definitions of what prosperity is for them.

However, there are certain things they do have in common. They all have a hungry enthusiasm for life and a positive attitude that they'll continue to use on the journey forward.

If you feel that you lack any of the core beliefs and are still unsure whether you can adopt a prosperity mindset, you could always look into getting advice from a coach. They'll be able to break down your problems and concerns and tailor a plan that will work for you personally.

When you implement these strategies, you'll gain a renewed prosperity mindset that will help you on your life journey.

Getting Help Is Not a Weakness

No man is an island. Or to put it another way, no one can get through this life alone. This is a fact that prideful and hard-headed people have been trying to prove wrong for centuries. But our feelings on the matter don't change the facts. *Humans are social beings, and we developed societies for a reason.* We came together and formed communities so we could support one another and help each other succeed. And yet many people still hold the limiting belief that asking for help is a sign of weakness or an admission of failure.

But this isn't true!

As former President Barack Obama once said, "Asking for help isn't a sign of weakness, it's a sign of strength. It shows you have the courage to admit when you don't know something, and to learn something new."

So, if you aren't doing as well as you would like after implementing what you learned in this book, don't be afraid to take the next step. *The most talented people in history had someone to train them, and you are no exception.*

As Bill Gates said in his 2013 TED Talk, "Everyone needs a coach. It doesn't matter whether you're a basketball player, a tennis player, a gymnast, or a bridge player. We all need people who will give us feedback. That's how we improve."

I have multiple coaches. I have a business coach to help me to build my business, a marketing coach to help me attract more clients, a financial coach to help me with my retirement savings plan, and two mindset coaches to help me along the journey written about in this book. These are a few examples to illustrate the investments I've made in my own journey. On the next page, you learn how these principles have impacted folks we've worked with.

Go to TimCampsall.com to learn more about our coaching and to have a business strategy coaching session.

__No matter how good you are at your job, you'd be better with a coach. Everyone needs one!__

— Eric Schmidt

Chairman & CEO of Google and

co-author of *Trillion Dollar Coach*

Client testimonials

KEVIN KINDER - OWNER OF INDY CRAFT PAINTING & STUDIO 342

Owning a small business has several challenges. You fix that for which you have time. This means there are many things you will not get around to fixing! The longer they go "unfixed," the harder they become to correct. My agreement with Tim was to coach me as a CEO of a larger corporation and not the owner of a small business. In other words, change the way I look at business. Not just my business, but business in general. What are larger companies doing that I am not?

The changes in my views and attitude are unmeasurable. It is simple, most everything you have learned in life was taught to you by a teacher or "coach." Why would building a business be an exception? I repeatedly hear the answer when asked about a business goal, "to increase my sales by X%." I immediately wonder if there is a plan in place to achieve and measure that. Sure, increasing sales by 10%, 20% or even 50% sounds great, right? But how do you get there? Simple solution here folks, ask Tim. So many of us business owners strive to rise above our competition. The "If you don't have time to do it right the first time, when will you have time to do it again" mentality definitely applies to building your business!

Working with Tim has completely changed my views as a business owner. My only regret is having not met him 30 years ago. It's never too late to hire a coach, BUT it also is never too soon.

CINDY NICKS - OWNER OF SUNSHINE CLEAN INDY

Hi, my name is Cynthia Nicks, and I am a "workaholic." Call me crazy but I love to work. I love helping others and being paid for it. When I met Tim, I basically had no goals or dreams, I just worked and paid the bills.

I basically had a "bad job," working many hours a week. I did not have a "business." Now after being coached by Tim through the principles in this book, I am actually "retiring" to the lake and my business is running without me. Making an income without working in the daily business is really a dream!!!! Hiring Tim, (and I am really a penny pincher) was a great investment. He not only helped my business grow BUT helped me as a person to grow and have more time to enjoy my family.

We business owners need to encourage each other and the best way for me to encourage you is to tell you to hire Tim as your coach.

ADAM JURS - OWNER OF JURS INSURANCE & FINANCIAL SERVICES, INC.

Coach Tim understands business, and more importantly, controlling the most important real estate that every human owns-the six inches between one's ears! All great leaders lead with their hearts, and our mind can be our best or worst enemy. Coach Tim helps break feelings down to what is reality vs. self-manifestation. He is not only one of the most trustworthy individuals I have met, he also cares truly about his client's success and takes the outcomes seriously.

Being an entrepreneur is not easy and there are consistent new challenges that will always need to be conquered! That's where Coach Tim has helped the most- being a critical-thinking partner to help control the emotional rollercoaster we can all face at times during our journey. It can be lonely at the top, and even with years of leadership experience. Having an outside perspective on our thoughts and feelings is something that everybody needs, no matter your successes in business. I highly recommend having an introductory call to find out how valuable his coaching can be!

Thank you for all you do, Coach.

JAMI GRAHAM - OWNER OF FENCE BOSS

After investing in Tim as my business coach, I reluctantly learned the importance of mindset as I completed coaching homework. I was accustomed to success via "hustle and muscle" and my workday usually involved putting out a large fire somewhere, or little fires everywhere. I celebrated success on the outside while I was exhausted on the inside.

I completed assigned coaching tasks thinking it was a waste of time.

I was busy and I wanted to work, I most certainly did not want to try to map out a detailed plan for the next 90 days. I was accustomed to succeeding at whatever I attempted via sheer grit and intellect. Planning was an annoyance and planning with flowery positive statements was a bigger annoyance. Nothing was tracked and measured so failure was rarely noticed or acknowledged. Consequently, I never learned to accept failure gracefully.

A year and a half into coaching my world turned on its axis when my youngest daughter nearly died and was left quadriplegic. I watched her stop breathing. I pleaded with the universe to save her life. I promised with fervor that I would never complain again if I could keep her.

For the first time, I faced a challenge I could not overcome with intellect and grit. At 50 years old I finally comprehended the importance of mindset. I promised my darling girl I would get her back on her feet and back to her life. I encouraged her every day and reminded her of the beautiful life ahead of her as she went through the grueling process of learning to walk and use her body again.

I spent 4-1/2 months out of the office living in various healthcare facilities with her. I returned to the business months later in a daze and $600,000 down in gross revenue. As a business owner, I had failed. Reliance on my own personal abilities, rather than a sound *plan and consistent structured processes had produced failure at a time when I needed my business the most.*

However, my mindset was new. I was no longer afraid to fail, I was surrounded by it in a mountain of collections and frustrated customers. Suddenly, I saw the depth of value in a positive mindset and consistent planning. I was determined to pull my business out of the ditch. I made a plan, and I took on one task at a time. After staring death in the face, nothing could penetrate my new positive mindset. One year later my business had forward momentum again and I was the positive planner in chief. My new motto is "Mindset is Everything."

TERI CAPRON - OWNER OF FRESH DESIGN

Using Tim and the ActionCOACH methods has helped me put processes in place and helped me see where my business is and where it is going. It is much easier to predict and plan.

These methods have allowed me as a business owner to look at my mindset and shake my thinking patterns so I'm no longer "stuck" or plateaued. I've been able to get to a place that eliminates or at the very least reduces the scarcity mindset and to bring a positive spin to how I look at projects for my clients. Because of this mindset, it brings more value to my clients by not having limiting beliefs holding my creativity back.

The quarterly planning meetings with Tim keep the accountability in place to make sure I stick to the plan I've developed. Also, it's been great to have the chance to meet other like-minded business owners at these meetings working to implement better systems, processes, and have measurable goals in place. We are able to share similar struggles and learn from each other which is a plus. It's not just coaching, it becomes a community.

Working "on" my business not just "in," has helped me to now have better clients that value what my business does for them and an increase in my income. Thanks to Tim for teaching me how to rethink, evaluate and monitor my business practices.

ANGELA PETERSON - OWNER OF HUPP JEWELERS

I became a business owner in the fall of 2018. And not because I wanted to own a business, but because I was fired from the job I held for 20 years; I bought myself a job from which I could not ever be fired!

My former job was so deeply embedded into who I was as a person, that I told the story of how unfairly I'd been treated to anyone who would listen. I met Tim through a business networking group, and we met to discuss how we could mutually benefit from each other's companies. And I told him my sad story. His response was "That's your past, what does your future hold?"

It has taken me almost 5 years to turn my mindset around. I thought the daily affirmations were stupid, I lived in a panic of making enough money to break even, not even believing I was good enough to thrive. Three things have changed my perspective.

1. *Tim told me to change my daily affirmations from "I am" statements to "I am becoming" statements. "I am wealthy beyond my wildest dreams" was obviously a lie, but... "I am BECOMING wealthy beyond my wildest dreams" makes a world of difference to me.*

2. *I found a daily calendar that was affirming and when the daily saying struck a nerve, I taped it to the wall in front of my desk, or the door jamb where I would see it and read it several times a day. For me, the most meaningful statement helped me resolve my past hurt and look toward my future. It said, "Your worth is not dependent on others' ability to see your value".*

3. *I found a phone app that sends me affirmations several times a day based on what I want to attract. You get to choose the categories, the frequency, the sayings, etc. I admit that when my phone dings, I am anxious to see who is texting and why. Even a glance at my phone is a boost to my confidence.*

I still struggle with making decisions based out of fear or feeling like I'm an imposter. But when I look back over the curve of the last 5 years I see the arc of earnings, I see the decisions made are sound and made (mostly) based on facts and not emotions. I see the correlation between my attitude and my earnings and, frankly, my joy in everyday life.

I don't think there is a formula that works for everyone but find what works for you. Keep looking until you find it then commit to it for a period that actually gives it time to work. If I can do it, you can too! Good Luck!

MELANIE MASSEY - CO-OWNER OF SPAULDING DECON INDIANAPOLIS

When I first met Tim, I was a pretty new business owner. I thought the only thing I really needed help with to grow my business was to learn marketing better. I figured I would either learn on my own or hire someone that knew how to do that better than I ever could.

Several months later, I found myself in the struggle of get the business, do the business, and honestly spending more time "in the business" than anything else. I was stressed and unsure how to take the next step. That's when I decided I needed more than marketing help and turned to Tim.

Since that time, I have learned so much - and have a lot more to go. What has changed the most has been my mindset, attitude, and stress level. Our business has faced more than the "typical" challenges, and several people in my same situation are struggling to stay positive. While I struggle with that too, I have been "above the point of power" more often than not. The concepts in this book that Tim uses in our coaching has helped me continue to march on and "be" a better person and business owner. This experience has been an investment not only to the business, but to me as a person. I can't thank Tim enough for the positive influence he has had on multiple aspects of my life!

"Self-reflection is the gateway to freedom. It also brings greater appreciation and enjoyment. We begin to enjoy spending time with our own mind, and we enjoy reflecting on our experience of the teachings. Like the sun emerging from behind the clouds, the teachings of the dharma become clear"

- Dzigar Kongrul Rinpoche

#6

Reflection Questions

Greatness

Are you achieving the level of success that you want? If not, where are you now?

Do you currently feel dissatisfied with any part of your life? Which parts?

What dreams and goals do you want to achieve? Do you believe that you can achieve them?

What is holding you back from reaching your full potential?

What do you think it takes to accumulate wealth?

Beliefs

On a scale of "terrible" to "excellent", how would you rate your relationship to money and why?

What long-standing beliefs do you have about making money?

76

Were you taught to see money as evil? Does your belief line up with the reality about money?

What do you think about those who want more money? Are your beliefs rational or correct?

What are some of the good things that you could accomplish if you made more money?

Limitations

How are limiting beliefs damaging?

What exactly is standing between you and happiness? Use this space to list all the obstacles that you believe are currently holding you down.

Brainstorm the beliefs you have, good and bad, regarding the challenges you just identified. Once you have finished, rank your beliefs from most damaging to least damaging.

Now that you have a list of the limiting beliefs that are holding you back, use this space to go through the elimination process below that we talked about in Part 3. Use the next couple pages to work through this exercise with each of your limiting beliefs from the previous page.

- Is this belief actually true?

- Where did this belief come from?

- Verbally tell yourself you no longer believe it.

- Come up with a new belief to replace the old one. What is it? How does it serve you rather than hold you back?

- How will you reflect your new belief in your daily actions?

Limiting Beliefs Elimination Process Exercise – Continued

81

Limiting Beliefs Elimination Process Exercise – Continued

82

After you've worked on implementing these new beliefs, come back to this page and reflect on the changes it has made in your life.

83

Mindset

Do you tend to focus most of your attention on positive or negative things?

Does your current mindset attract the wealth and success that you desire? Why do you think that is?

What level of control do you have over your "inner world" (thoughts, desires, and dreams)? How can you strengthen your control?

Do you have a scarcity or abundance mindset when it comes to money? Which traits from Part 4 do you exhibit in your life?

Why is the scarcity mindset so unhelpful when it comes to achieving success and generating wealth?

What is the "wealth principle," and how does it lead to massive success?

What are some simple ways you can begin practicing gratitude right now?

Why is taking action so critically important?

Write down your main goal in the space below. Then break it down into steps and set manageable goals.

What roadblocks might slow you down in your journey? How will you adapt your plan if these problems come to pass?

What action can you take today?

List some successful people you admire. What did they do to become successful? What mistakes did they make along the way? How can you apply this to your own journey?

"Don't be pushed around by the fears in your mind. Be led by the dreams in your heart."

- Roy T. Bennett

The Light in the Heart

#7

Millionaire Mindset Affirmations

Here are some suggested affirmations to use to get you started. As you build the muscle and create the habit, you should tailor these with ones that are more specific to your own journey.

I want to have more money and that does not make me a bad person.

Money is neutral. What matters most is what I choose to do with my money.

I can do a lot of good with the wealth I accumulate.

I am generous, big-hearted, and ready to help anyone in need. Wealth naturally flows to me, and as a result, I am grateful. I am grateful to my Creator for His abundant graces and generosity.

I know that there is abundance in the world, and I choose to receive that abundance.

I refuse to let past beliefs keep me from getting the wealth that I deserve.

I reject any myths that I have believed that needlessly limited me. I embrace my natural greatness and attract good things.

I make more than enough money.

When I make any money, I am filled with gratitude. I say, "Thank you," for even the smallest amounts of money, because gratitude fills me with joy and attracts more good things into my life.

Money is a good thing and I make more than enough. I am a wealth magnet.

I choose to focus on abundance.

My mind is incredibly powerful.

What I give my attention to grows. What I focus on expands. My mind controls the outcomes that I experience in my life.

I have a mindset of abundance.

I attract positive things because I constantly think about positive things. My outer life is extremely positive because my inner life is also extremely positive.

Because I focus on good things, I attract good things into my life.

I attract wealth, goodness, and beauty. I gratefully receive the abundance that the Creator provides me.

There is more than enough for every person in the

world, including me…

…and I choose to receive what is rightfully mine. Because I believe in abundance, I manifest abundance wherever I go and in whatever I do.

I know that my Creator has my back.

They are constantly looking for ways to bring good into my life. I simply must open myself up to the endless possibilities the Creator offers me. I live life to the fullest, enjoying and exploring all the amazing opportunities that come my way.

And because the Creator has my back, I am grateful.

I receive wealth and blessings with open hands, thankful for all that I am receiving.

I take action on my dreams.

Today, I choose to take massive action on my dreams. I know that when I combine my abundance mindset with massive action, I truly achieve limitless results. I avoid waiting for things to happen. Instead, I will make them happen.

I am capable of achieving my biggest dreams.

Nothing can stop me because I am relentless in pursuing them. I know the Creator has my back. This belief gives me great confidence as I pursue my goals and seek to accumulate wealth.

What I focus on becomes a reality, and I am laser-focused on my dreams.

I control all my thoughts and use them to push me toward achieving my dreams. My thoughts lead to my feelings, which lead to my actions, which lead to my reality.

I affirm that this will be my financially best year so far. I will hit all my financial goals. I attract the wealth that I desire and deserve. I am a financial success in every area of my life.

I know that I attract abundance, and when I combine abundance with action, amazing things happen.

I am excited to see all the good things happening in my life. I keep pushing and striving until I reach the success that I desire, and my dreams come true.

About The Author

Tim Campsall is an author, international speaker/trainer, global award-winning coach and certified as a business and executive coach.

He has helped over 700 business professionals both with professional/ personal growth and business growth.

Prior to owning an ActionCOACH® franchise, Tim spent over 20 years in the corporate world running businesses and coaching leaders/teams.

Tim was born and raised in Canada and moved to the U.S. in 2005 as part of a career advancement. He is married to his amazing wife Petrita and has three step-boys.

Tim enjoys traveling, growing vegetables in his garden and hosting parties and events.

To learn more about Tim, to book him for a speaking event or to schedule a meeting with him about mindset or coaching go to TimCampsall.com